POCKET IMAGES

Wetherby

The Town Hall in 1845 as it was, first designed and built at a cost of £1,300.

POCKET IMAGES

Wetherby

Wetherby & District Historical Society

NONSUCH

First published 1995
This new pocket edition 2007
Images unchanged from first edition

Nonsuch Publishing Limited
Cirencester Road, Chalford,
Stroud, Gloucestershire, GL6 8PE
www.nonsuch-publishing.com

Nonsuch Publishing is an imprint of NPI Media Group

British Library Cataloguing in Publication Data.
A catalogue record for this book is available from the British Library.

ISBN 978-1-84588-395-9

Typesetting and origination by Nonsuch Publishing Limited
Printed in Great Britain by Oaklands Book Services Limited

Contents

Acknowledgements

Grateful thanks to:

The Town Mayor Mrs S Evans, Mr M Bale, Mrs M Bentham, Mr R Hall, Mr D Kitchen, Dr J Lodge, Mr G Stott, Mrs B Wilson and to everyone in Wetherby who gave so freely of their pictures, time and knowledge.

Introduction

Most towns or localities pride themselves on having a unique feature or attribute, something particular associated with them that distinguishes them from other towns or areas. Wetherby's claim to be different is that, as far as is known, it is the only town to have been sold in its entirety! This came about in 1824 when the 6th Duke of Devonshire, who owned almost all the town and much of the surrounding land, found himself in need of money. Whether this was to pay his gambling debts, as one story goes, or to fund work at Chatsworth is not known, but the sum required was great enough to persuade him to sell all his property in the area. The sale raised over £250,000, a very large sum in those days. The catalogue issued for the sale gives a snapshot of Wetherby at a particular moment in its history and is an extremely valuable document for anyone researching the history of the town.

However, Wetherby did not spring into being fully formed in 1824. People have lived, and died, by the crossing of the Wharfe since Roman times. The Saxons knew the small settlement as Wederbi. Later the Knights Templars had a small castle overlooking the river bridge and their obtaining of a Market Charter in 1240 shows that Wetherby was already becoming the focal point for the farms and villages in the surrounding area. The Scots came calling with plunder in mind and there are stories of blood running in the streets. During the Civil War the town was held for Parliament by the Fairfaxes and in 1642 a Royalist force from York tried to seize the bridge but was driven off after a short battle.

Situated on the Great North Road, Wetherby has always been a busy place. In earlier times, spring and autumn saw the town thronged with droves of cattle whilst, throughout the coaching age, both mail and stage coaches stopped regularly at the various inns in the town. The coaches were followed by the railways. The main lines passed east and west of Wetherby which became a quieter place, but the growth of the motor traffic after the 1914-18 War saw the town once more humming with vehicles; although nowadays, since the by-pass was built, most of the traffic is local, trying to cross High Street or the Market Place gives some idea of what it was like in days gone by.

The photographs in this book cover approximately a hundred years and while they are a graphic illustration of how Wetherby, like most British towns, has changed physically they also recall the people, their sports and pastimes and the events that shaped their lives during the past century.

Monday 11 October 1824, the day Wetherby came under the hammer.

One

The Duke of Devonshire's Great Sale of 1824

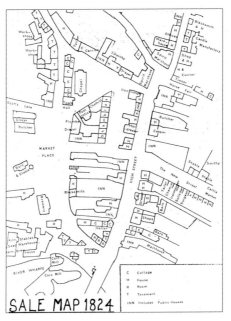

SALE MAP 1824

This map was used to identify the properties
included in the sale. Only one property was
excluded.

YORKSHIRE.

THE
Whole Town of Wetherby,
MANOR AND ESTATE OF 1300 ACRES.

Specifications
OF A CAPITAL AND EXTENSIVE
FREEHOLD ESTATE,
CONSISTING OF THE WHOLE OF
THE TOWN OF WETHERBY,
In the County of York,

Situate on the high Turnpike Road by FERRY BRIDGE to GLASGOW, distant from LEEDS 12 Miles, YORK 14, and FERRY BRIDGE 12 Miles; comprising

TWO POSTING HOUSES, THREE INNS, SEVEN PUBLIC HOUSES,
EXTENSIVE WATER CORN MILLS, BREWERY, WAREHOUSES,
AND NEARLY
TWO HUNDRED DWELLING HOUSES,
WITH SEVERAL
ELIGIBLE SCITES FOR BUILDING,
On the Banks of the very beautiful River WHARFE,
Which Bounds the Estate for about One Mile and a Half.

ALSO,
The Valuable Manor of Wetherby,
COEXTENSIVE WITH THE TOWNSHIP,

With Courts Baron and Leet, Quit Rents, Tolls of Fairs, the Stallage and Piccage of the Markets, Rents and Profits of the Shambles, and all other Rights, Members, and Appurtenances thereto belonging;
TOGETHER WITH
Upwards of 1300 Acres,
COMPRISING
ALL THE DESIRABLE FARMS & LANDS,
Most advantageously situate, contiguous to and entirely surrounding the Town;
THE WHOLE OF WHICH DESIRABLE PROPERTY IS IN THE OCCUPATION OF YEARLY TENANTS,
AND IS OF THE ESTIMATED VALUE OF NEARLY
Five Thousand Pounds per Annum:
Which will be Sold by Auction,

BY MR. DRIVER,
at WETHERBY,
On MONDAY, the 11th OCTOBER, 1824, and Three following Days,
AT ELEVEN O'CLOCK EACH DAY,
In 170 Lots.

Printed Specifications, with Plans annexed, to be had at the *Angel* and *Swan* Inns, Wetherby; York Tavern, and the George, York; the Hotel, and the Kings Arms, Leeds; the Granby, Harrowgate; the Angel, Ferrybridge; of Mr. ROBERT DICKSON, Londesborough, near Market Weighton; at the Auction Mart, London; and of Messrs. DRIVER, Surveyors and Land Agents, 13, New Bridge Street, Blackfriars, London.

First page of the 1824 sale catalogue.

Specifications.

THE FOLLOWING

IMPORTANT PROPERTY IS ALL FREEHOLD,

AND COMPRISES THE

Whole of the large Market Town of Wetherby,

(WITH THE EXCEPTION OF ONLY ONE HOUSE THEREIN,)

AS WELL AS

THE MANOR,

WHICH IS COEXTENSIVE WITH THE TOWNSHIP;

INCLUDING THE TOLLS OF ALL FAIRS,

AND THE

Stallage and Pickage of the Markets;

AND ALSO, ALL THE

SURROUNDING LAND AND FARMS,

COMPRISING

Above 1300 Acres,

CONTIGUOUS TO THE TOWN ON ALL SIDES.

The *Town of Wetherby* is on the high Turnpike Road by *Ferry Bridge* to *Glasgow,* and, in the direct line of communication between *Leeds* and *York;* and very considerable advantages are expected to this Town, from the New Turnpike Road now in progress from *Leeds,* to pass through *Wetherby,* by which there will be a saving of nearly Four Miles in distance between these Towns; and a new line of Turnpike Road from *Wetherby* is projected to pass through this Estate towards *York,* which will shortly offer additional advantages and benefits to the Town and Neighbourhood, by saving a further distance between *Wetherby* and *York.*

Wetherby is central to the following Places, and distant about 16 Miles from *Fe____* ... from *Tadcaster* ; 12 from *Leeds* ; 8 from *Harrow____* ... ough.

The beautiful River W____ ... Town of *Wetherby,* and forms the Boundary of the Estate for ____ about One Mile and a Half; and upon its Banks, which are in most places peculiarly Beautiful and Picturesque, there are many delightful Scites for Building.

Upon the River there are Two extensive CORN MILLS belonging to this Estate, and included in this Particular.

The town was identified as an important stop on the High Turnpike Road by Ferry Bridge and Glasgow.

THE HOUSES AND PREMISES

TOWN OF WETHERBY.

MONDAY, the 11th Day of OCTOBER, 1824.

LOT 1.

No.	Occupiers.		Description.
120	William Hind	.....	THE SWAN and TALBOT INN and POSTING HOUSE, in the High Street, containing on the GROUND FLOOR, Five Rooms, (exclusive of Bar,) Kitchen, Back Kitchen, Larder, Soldier's Room, Eight best Bed Rooms, and Five Servant's Rooms. In the Yard is a POST HORSE STABLE for 11 Horses, 2 open Stables, Cowhouse, a Lumber Room formerly a Malt Kiln, Hay chamber over, Coach house, Coal and Bottle Houses, with Stack Garth and Garden, containing 0A. 2R. 18P.
			A large Garden on the opposite side of the road containing 0A. 2R. 16P. with a Stone Building known as the Old Court House, comprising the Court Room and Two Rooms adjoining, a 7 Stall Stable underneath, Granary behind the Court Room, a Bailed Stable for 4 Horses with Granary over, and a Dove Cote.
405	Ditto	.....	A small part of the Field adjoining the Stable, containing 0A. 0R. 10P.

To be Fenced off by the Purchaser of this Lot:

John Clemershow
1510

LOT 2.

190a	William Hind	.....	A stone Building, tiled, fronting the High Street, comprising 2 Stables for 12 Horses, with Lofts over.
Pt. of 122	Henry Smith	....	Part of a Garden behind ditto.
Pt. of 123	George Newstead		Part of another Garden.

The Purchaser of this Lot to Fence against Lots 3 and 5.

John Smith
235

LOT 3.

121c	John Hawkes	.....	A DWELLING HOUSE in the Yard, and a Blacksmith's Shop in the High Street
121a	James Weather		tenement in front.
121b	John Ellice		
121d	Joseph Askwith		factory, a Yard, Barn, Cowhouse; Pig Cot, Stable, &c.
121e	William Grainger		h Street.
Pt. 122	Henry Smith		

Joseph Asgwith £15

LOT 4.

121d	Joseph Askwith	.....	A good DWELLING HOUSE and Shop in High Street, with 2 Kitchens, Parlor, 4 Chambers, Granary, Cellar, and Yard behind.

£300

B

The Swan and Talbot sold for £1,510 with nine outbuildings, plus the garden and another building across the road.

SECOND DAY'S SALE.

TUESDAY, the 12th Day of OCTOBER, 1824.

LOT 48.

No.	Occupiers.	Description:
66	Widow Smith	The CROWN INN, in High-Street, containing on the GROUND FLOOR, Two Parlors, Dining Room, a Back Room, Bar and Scullery; Cellar, Four Bedchambers and a small Room: In the Yard is a Brewhouse, Store Room, Coal House, Barn, Cow House, Pig Cotes, a Seven Stall Stable with Granary over; another Stable with a Malt Room over, and a Box Stable. These Premises extend back into the Market Place.

£ 1040

LOT 49

62	George Atkinson	A good DWELLING-HOUSE in the High Street, containing on the GROUND FLOOR, a Sitting Room, Two Parlors, Kitchen and small Back Room, and Three Bedchambers; a Yard behind, communicating with the Market Place, in which is a covered Well, Coal House, Pig Cotes, Barn, Cow House, and Seven Stall Stabling with Granary over.
63 & 65	Samuel Wiggins	A small Shop and Loft fronting the Market Place.
	Ann Fisher	A Room.

£??

LOT 50.

61	Widow Hargrave ..	The RED LION Public House in High Street, containing on the GROUND FLOOR, Small Parlor, Dining Room, and another Parlor; Two Kitchens, Bar, Pantry and Back Room adjoining; Dairy, Coal Hole, and Two Cellars, and Seven Bed Chambers. In the Yard which communicates with the Market Place is a covered Well, a Soldiers Room, and Granary over; a Two-stall Stable with Granary over, another Stable with Three Stalls, and Three large open Stables with Hay Chambers. Another open Stable, Granary, and a small Garden.
58	Thomas Smith ..	A Smithy and Iron Chamber over, in front next the Market Place.
60	Thomas Smith..	A DWELLING HOUSE in the High Street.
59	Samuel Wiggins	A DWELLING HOUSE fronting the Market Place, with a Stable behind and Chamber over.

Mr Jackson 1870

LOT 51.

57	Jane Greaves	The BLUE BOAR Public House in High Street, containing Two Parlors, Kitchen, Back Kitchen, Two Cellars, and Four Chambers. In the Yard, which communicates with the Market Place, is a Brewhouse, and Two open Stables with Granary and Hay Chamber over.

Mr ??der 660

D

On the second day of the sale, three inns were sold: The Crown, The Red Lion and The Blue Boar for a total price of £2,870.

LOT 5.

No.	Occupiers.		Description.
122	Henry Smith	....	A capital Brick built DWELLING HOUSE in High Street, containing 2 Parlors, Kitchen, Wash house, Dairy, 4 Chambers, and 2 Garrets. A Yard containing a Curriers Workshop and Chamber over, Warehouse, Drying Shed, a new 2 stall Stable, Garden and Orchard.
123	George Newstead	....	Part of a DWELLING HOUSE, in High Street, containing Shop, 2 Sitting Rooms, Kitchen, Work Shop, 3 Chambers and 2 Lofts. Another DWELLING HOUSE in the Horse Fair, in the occupation of Mrs. *Newstead.*—A Yard behind, with Cow House, Hay Chamber over, Shed, Pig Cot, Garden, and part of Orchard.

(£20)

LOT 6.

124b	Thomas Varley	.....	A DWELLING HOUSE in Horse Fair. An Orchard behind with Cowhouse and Stable.
a	Ann Whitfield	......	A Cottage
c	William Wardall	...	Ditto
d	Ruth Whitfield	...	Ditto
e	William Scott	...	Ditto
f	William Greaves	...	Ditto

LOT 7.

126	John Clemishaw	....	The ANGEL INN and POSTING HOUSE, in the High Street, being a large Brick-built House, containing on the GROUND FLOOR Five Rooms, besides the Bar and Kitchen, 7 best Bed Chambers, 5 other Rooms, and Laundry over the Kitchen. A spacious Yard containing Coal House, Harness Room, Ostrey, Stall-Stabling for 17 Horses, open Stable for 14 Post Horses with Granary and Hay Chamber over, Standing for 3 Carriages and Soldiers Room over, another Stable with 4 Stalls and Hay Loft over. In the Outer Yard a large Barn, Range of Cowhouses, Stables, &c. round the Fold Yard.
127	Jonathan Arrowsmith		A DWELLING HOUSE adjoining, 3 Stories high, containing 2 Rooms on the Ground Floor, and 3 Rooms on each Floor above Cellars.—One Room of this House is occupied with The ANGEL, and used as a Dairy.

LOT 8.

131	In hand	......	The DEVONSHIRE ARMS INN, in High Street, a substantial New Stone-Built House, slated, containing on the GROUND FLOOR, Two Parlours in Front, Bar, Kitchen, Scullery, and Cellar; on the FIRST FLOOR, a large Room in front, used as an Assembly Room, and 3 good Bed Chambers. On the SECOND FLOOR, ... Garret, and a Dark Room in an Inner Yard; and ... uge of newly erected Stable Buildings Tiled, comp... Standing for Two Carriages; a 4-Stall Stable and ... for 8 Horses, with Granaries and Lofts over the whole...
130	Samuel Wiggins	......	A DWELLING HOUSE in the High Street, now used as a Cooper's Shop. A Yard behind; with a new Tiled Barn, Cow-house; also another Yard used by *William Hill,* as a communication with some Premises adjoining.
131 & 132	John Walker	......	Two Stone Built Stables and Ground behind, fronting the New Street.

This describes properties in Horse Fair complete with cow-house, stable and orchard.

Two

Wetherby and the Wharfe

Wetherby bridge as it appeared in an early engraving published in 1829. There has been some artistic licence taken. It is obvious that the painting was done prior to the second downstream widening in 1826. The original bridge of c.1220 was only 11 feet wide with a marked hump; this was lowered during the 1773 upstream widening.

MICKLETHWAITE.   *Crossley, Wetherby.*

Micklethwaite prior to 1905. The building on the left was the Drover Inn. Cattle pastured outside the town had to pass in order to get over Wetherby bridge. With the advent of the railway, cattle were no longer herded past the Drovers Inn and the name changed to the Spotted Ox. Note the barracks with its flagpole built c.1825 to house the Yorkshire Hussars stationed there in case of civil disturbance at nearby Leeds, for instance during the troubled times of the Chartists.

Wetherby Bridge.

Looking south over Wetherby bridge towards Micklethwaite Farm. The farm workers cottages behind the railings still exist as a private residence.

A view of the weir showing the Old Mill and Brewery. It can be seen that this picture shows the fire ravaged Mill undemolished. The private residence behind the Mill ruins housed the first Nonconformist services and Quaker Meetings in Wetherby c.1689.

The weir showing the Mill raceway. Also it can be seen that some of the Mill buildings were being used as a sawmill.

Wetherby bridge featuring the telephone pole erected in 1910 and which today bears the town's Coat of Arms. Behind the pole can be seen Bishopsgate (now Bridge Foot). The Bishop was probably Walter De Gray, Archbishop of York who gave an indulgence (i.e. remission of temporal punishment due for sins already committed and repeated) to those who contributed to the cost of construction of the Bridge at Werreby in 1233.

The river and bridge taken from the Wilderness, c.1910, also giving a good view of the brewery.

Above: Wharfedale Brewery, c.1910. Note the ornate chimney and surrounding buildings. Over the years the brewery supplied ale to many of the town's 15 inns. When it closed during the First World War it provided billets for the troops with their horses being housed in the brewery stables. Later it became Oxley's mineral water factory and when the American troops arrived in 1943 Coca Cola was manufactured from concentrates imported from America. At the end of the Second World War the Brewery offices were used by the West Yorkshire Bus Company as a booking office. These premises were later demolished to make way for a modern bus station.

Right: The end of an era was marked by the demolition of a major landmark, the brewery chimney in 1959.

The West End boating stage which is now a restaurant shows Richmond's working shed erected c.1930. The lower level was used to dry out cushions whilst the top area provided repair facilities.

Tom Richmond's West End boating stage c.1928 offering rowing, punting and Canadian style skiffs. Large numbers of people came from Leeds by bus to Wetherby to enjoy a day on the river. The young man was known locally as Jim Kitchen.

Tom Richmond's motor boat, c.1930. At weekends he offered regular trips from the West End boating stage up as far as Collingham Bridge. Large numbers of organisations from Leeds would regularly book trips.

The river Wharfe at Scaur Bank c.1930, shows a typical boating party of young university students enjoying a pleasant afternoon watched by their parents.

Linton Ings viewed from the top of Scaur Bank. In 1842 Lord Leconfield was persuaded to allow horse racing to be run over the Wetherby and Linton Ings, the four mile course extending in a loop between both parishes. The slope of the foreground steps formed a natural amphitheatre being ideal for spectators. Grandstands were erected there with a hundred plush chairs which were let out for ladies at a cost of £1 each for the Meeting, a large amount of money at that time. The cavalry regiments including the Dragoons, who were stationed at Wetherby, provided most of the horses and riders. All the races had been steeplechases and in March 1865 the 1st Yorkshire Grand National was run there with the jockeys having to be gentlemen farmers or their sons; it was watched by 30,000 people. The opening of the Leeds/Wetherby railway in 1876 resulted in the shortening of the course. However, fashions changed and horse racing declined in popularity with the last race being run there on Easter Tuesday 1890. This land is now used for leisure facilities. The archway was built to commemorate the Silver Jubilee of King George V and the playing fields took King George's name.

A winter scene of Wetherby bridge in 1963.

Wentworth Terrace across the frozen river Wharfe in the winter of 1963. The ice was so thick that the Wetherby Silver Band came and played to the skaters on the ice.

This fine bridge built in the late 1950s to carry traffic over the Wharfe as part of the town by-pass was officially opened by the then Minister of Transport, Ernest Marples.

The river Wharfe bridge and Mill site during the floods of February 1995. It can be noted that the weir almost disappeared under the flood water.

Three

The Market Town

Market day at the beginning of the twentieth century. Notice the bell between the chimneys used to call the part-time fire brigade.

Market day in front of the Town Hall, c.1910. Note the horses and the baskets used for bringing local produce for sale.

The market on the south side of the Town Hall, c.1904. Note that as well as the stalls around the Town Hall, produce was sold from trestle tables along the pavement. This whole area was private land belonging to the Lord of the Manor, Andrew Montagu of Ingmanthorpe Hall.

The east side of the Market Place c.1910. The side door to the Town Hall enabled prisoners to be taken safely to the Court in the upper room. Wilsons' grocers reveals a low arch for horse-drawn deliveries.

The Magistrates Court was held in the Town Hall from 1845 until 1982; here we can see the Bench and the Dock.

The Market Place looking North, c.1905. Notice the only traffic is one horse-drawn cart and it is easy to understand how the local boys could play cricket against the Town Hall wall with chalk wickets and no wicket-keeper.

A similar view 50 years later on a market day with a lot more traffic evident. The building on the right being the office of Coates and Bretts, Solicitors, said to have been the oldest house in the town having survived the 1723 fire which destroyed over half the buildings in the town centre. Note the Town Hall has lost its tall chimneys with the movement from coal-fired heating.

The Town Hall and Barclays Bank with the new electric lighting of 1962.

The Church.

Old Market Shambles Wetherby.

The Old Market Shambles, previously butchers shops, were converted to a Market Hall by public subscription in 1911.

The north side of the Market Place showing Church Street locally known as the "Stumps" due to the two wooden stumps seen at the entrance. The two small girls are standing outside the premises of J R Hall, basket maker and corn dealer (now Renton and Parr). The gentleman with the straw boater is standing outside the house and small shop owned by Mr & Mrs Meeks.

A view of the Market Place, c.1910, looking towards the river bridge. The absence of traffic enabled children to play in the middle of the road; clearly shown is the central telegraph pole which has been retained to this day and bears the town's Coat of Arms.

Victoria Street, Monday cattle market c.1900. Note the carriages in front of the Brunswick Inn.

By 1900 the cattle market had extended into the High Street completely blocking the road which at that time was still the Great North Road. The clearly visible manure had considerable financial value. The Parish Council annually auctioned the right to collect it to the highest bidder thus producing an economical way of keeping the road clean.

The Little Fruit Shop at the junction of Cross Street and Market Place, c.1935. Notice the large and unusual advertisement which would now be illegal. Due to the distance of the railway station from the town centre, rail timetables were prominently displayed.

The same shop when it later became known as Ward's Newsagents.

The interior of Hills druggist shop as it was in 1924. Notice the old pestle and mortar, the very fine storage jars and the loving cup. Just why the stone (dated 1661) is there is unknown, since it is thought to have come from the old Chapel or Ease which was demolished to allow for the building of the Town Hall.

Wetherby & District CONSERVATIVE CLUB Ltd.

Scale of CHARGES for the use of a large ROOM in the above Club.

From 2-30 p.m. to 6-0 p.m. 5/-

After 6 p.m. for each additional hour up
to 8 p.m.—1/6 per hour.

The above scale of charges includes
Lighting and Heating.

Please apply to the Steward of the Club,
Mr. H. Pratt, for any particulars.

Above: The Conservative Club built on the site of the Devonshire Arms Inn; named after the Duke who owned the town of Wetherby until the Great Sale of 1824. In 1890 the Conservative Association purchased it to build the current structure at a cost of £1,176.9s.10d. The building became better known for beer and billiards rather than for its political activity. Notice the smartness of the policeman crossing the road.

Left: In 1950 the Club was having difficulties in paying its way and offered rooms to let. This long-term financial problem together with a dishonest steward led to its closure in 1958.

Above: Hall's ironmongers and tinners on High Street c.1910. Many of the tinsmith's tools from this shop are housed in the York Castle Museum collection.

Right: The advert of the day shows the wide variety of items sold at Hugh Hall's shop.

All requisites in Household Ironmongery Brooms, Brushes, Cutlery.

HUGH HALL

IRONMONGER AND TINNER.

Enamelled Ironware, Paints, Wringers, Carpet Sweepers.

Tin Goods Repaired and Coppers Re-tinned.

DEPOT FOR

LAMPS AND JOINERS' TOOLS OF ALL KINDS.

HIGH STREET, WETHERBY.

Guns and Cartridges. Netting. Garden Tools.

3

Above: The Market Place post office, c.1910. The strange object on the roof was part of the telephone exchange. The building to the left was a lodging house for down and outs and later became the Wetherby Whaler fish restaurant. The building to the right was the blacksmith shop of John Precious. It was alleged that he was the oldest working blacksmith in the country.

Opposite below: The Crossley Street shop of A T Ingles displaying in the window the familiar packets of Corn Flakes, All Bran and Weetabix. Also note the prominent tobacco advertising.

Right: The first fish and chip shop in Wetherby opened in the early 1920s by Mr & Mrs John Waterhouse.

Below: Moon's grocers (now Panache) on the High Street. This was the first shop in Wetherby to have electricity. The gentleman on the right was Mr Hogg.

General and Fancy
Drapers.

W. C. Woolliscroft

CLOTHIER
and OUTFITTER.

The Latest Styles in Millinery.

NEW GOODS
EVERY WEEK.

North St., Wetherby.

New
Range of Dress
Materials. The Newest Goods in the
Most Attractive Styles.

Opposite: Woolliscroft, clothiers and outfitters of North Street Wetherby.

Right: The shop of Mrs Harry Garforth in Bishopsgate facing the George and Dragon Inn c.1910. The little girl in the doorway later became Mrs Frost.

Below: This picture shows J. Wilson as a tea dealer; a very important commodity and quite expensive. It is recorded that very little coffee was drunk in rural Wetherby at this time.

Telephone—Wetherby, 2X ; Boston Spa, 1X.

TOPHAM & SONS

———— **high=class** ————

Decorators and Painters,

WETHERBY.

TOPHAM & SONS
HIGH CLASS PAINTERS & DECORATORS

BRANCHES AT BOSTON SPA & TADCASTER
& IN CONNECTION WITH TOPHAM & SONS, RIPON & THIRSK

Left: Topham's, high class painters and decorators, situated on the west side of the Market Place.

Below: These pseudo Elizabethan buildings stood at the junction of North Street and the Horsefair, c.1960. They were occupied by Teasdale and Metcalfe, Denham's the butcher and Mrs Ward. The firm of Teasdale and Metcalfe initially sold tractors and agricultural machinery in what had been a garage. However, they made their mark as constructional engineers producing Dutch barns still visible from Aberdeen to Truro and recognisable by the firm's familiar logo. Ultimately they became the largest employer of labour after the District Council.

North Street, Wetherby
junction with
Horsefair, October 1962

TEASDALE
& METCALFE LTD
CONSTRUCTIONAL
ENGINEERS

INDUSTRIAL BUILDINGS.
DUTCH BARNS.
FOLD YARDS.
FABRICATED STEELWORK.

Four

Ins and Outs of Wetherby

An aerial view of the town.

An early view of the bridge and Bishopsgate taken before Rose's shop was opened.

A view showing Bishopsgate with Rose's grocers shop, now demolished.

DEIGHTON ROAD, WETHERBY.

Deighton Road looking south, c.1912; the Great North Road at this stage was still unmetalled.

North End, Wetherby.

An attractive view of North End Wetherby.

Looking northwards along North Street from outside Swan House c.1908. Notice the church gates with their ornately capped pillars; even though this was the Great North Road it was quiet enough to drive a bullock down its centre.

Cattle and sheep being driven to market down North Street.

High Street, c.1900 with horse-drawn traffic, these buildings have hardly changed to this day. The Claro and Knaresborough Bank on the right is now the National Westminster Bank.

The narrowest point of the Great North Road between London and Edinburgh c.1910. Note the old Bowling Green Hotel on the left, later demolished for road widening.

A view of Westgate from St Joseph's R.C. church, c.1910. Notice the well dressed children standing in what is now the entrance to the Council Office car park. Behind the children is a box tree which at that time was extremely rare. The building in the centre with the wall lamp and flagpole was the Police Station built in 1861/2 and used until 1962.

An interesting scene of rural life in North Street. What a fine hat the lady on the left is wearing.

North Street Primitive Methodist chapel, c.1920. This view looks south towards the Manor House and the gates of St James's church.

The York Road junction, c.1930, showing the Convent in the centre. Notice the gas lighting and the rather less obtrusive telephone box.

Dalby's garage which previously had horse-drawn carriages for hire along with stabling for horses.

Looking south down North Street towards the Angel Hotel c.1935. On the left is Swan House and the Swan and Talbot Hotel. The building next to the hotel was then the solicitor's office of Bickers, Peters and Heap. Note the Manor House just visible beyond the stone wall on the right.

Looking north up High Street during the early part of the twentieth century. Notice the children on the left are still able to play on what is now a very busy thoroughfare.

A view up High Street from the north end of the bridge c.1921 showing the prominent and striking War Memorial consecrated in that year.

WETHERBY.

Wm. WARD & SONS,

Automobile Engineers.

Official Repairers to the Royal Automobile Club, A.A. and M.U., and leading Insurance Companies.

Power Plant, Examination Pits. Vulcanizing. Accumulators Charged.
Cylinders re-ground, Pistons & rings fitted by our own exclusive process.

Garage : Angel Yard and Horsefair.

Office and Showrooms : North Street.

Motor Accessories and Sundries. Petrol, Oils, and Greases.
Cars for Hire and Towing Purposes.

Dunlop Tyre Depot.

Michelin, Skew, Prowodnik, and Leading Makes of Tyres.

Sole District Agents for Triumph, P. and M., Rover, Bradbury, New Hudson, B.S.A., Torpedo, and other Motors.

Telephone 6X.

6

An interesting page from an advert showing details of Wm. Ward's garage and the wide range of services offered.

50

A quiet view of North Street after the 1929 road widening scheme, showing the Garden of Rest on the site of the demolished Bowling Green Inn.

A view of the town in 1905 from Raby Park.

A view showing the advance of Dalby's garage to the age of motoring. At this time the garage also ran the local ambulance service. Like many people they lived at their place of work, which was the house next door to the left of the petrol pumps.

Looking south down North Street in the early 1960s. Even by this date cars are few and far between.

High Street looking north towards the Midland Bank; there has been little change to the buildings although there have been changes to the retailing businesses.

Looking down Westgate towards the Market Place. The right-hand side of the road has now changed with many new buildings, including the library.

Deighton Road looking south towards the railway bridge demolished in 1962. Notice Dunlop and Ranken's advertisement on the bridge and the electric lamp standards in front of Waudby's garage and filling station. There has been very little change other than the trees in the garden of "Stone Dene".

The modernised southern approach to the town showing the bus station, which replaced the old brewery buildings.

Five

The Racecourse

ENTRANCE RACECOURSE, WETHERBY.

There has been racing in and around Wetherby at Clifford Moor, the "Bottoms" opposite Grange Park, Park Hill, Wetherby and Linton Ings and the current course since 1683. The present site held its first race on Easter Monday, March 30 1891 and has been home to the Bramham Moor Point-to-Point and hosts many of the Pony Club Shows and Events during the off-season. This photograph, taken in 1910, shows a very unnoticeable entrance to the Race Course from the unmetalled York Road.

The Stands, Wetherby Racecourse.

The stands at Wetherby have been modified several times. The one shown was completed in 1922 and remained the same until 1967 when new stands were erected.

THE WEIGHING ROOM, WETHERBY.

The Weighing Room in front of the Main Grand Stand.

The Princess Royal attending a 1923 Race Meeting. It was reported that the staff in the "Ladies" were asked to warm the seat for her.

Racing of a different kind, showing a "Brequet" aircraft which appears to have fallen at the first fence. In 1911 the racecourse was one of the stages for the Daily Mail £10,000 Circuit of Britain Air Race.

Picnicking on Wetherby Racecourse, 1907.

The Paddock crowd during the Whit Monday Meeting of 1937.

Stewards examining the dry ditch prior to the Easter Meeting of 1937.

CROSSLEY'S OFFICIAL PROGRAMME

× OF THE ×

WETHERBY ANNUAL

Steeplechases & Hurdle Races,

Easter Monday, April 16th, 1906,

Under National Hunt Rules.

Patrons.

RIGHT HON. LORD HAWKE.
RIGHT HON. LORD FABER.
SIR NEVILL GUNTER, Bart.
T. L. WICKHAM-BOYNTON, Esq.
GEORGE GUNTER, Esq.
C. B. LAMB, Esq.
MAJOR PLATT.
    F. J. O. MONTAGU, Esq.

R. J. FOSTER, Esq.
MAJOR COLLINS.
G. D. FABER, Esq., M.P.
E. W. STANYFORTH, Esq.
J. S. CHARLESWORTH, Esq.
COL. MEYSEY-THOMPSON.
J. FIELDEN, Esq.

Stewards.

RIGHT HON. THE EARL OF
    HAREWOOD.
CAPT. W. HOPE JOHNSTONE.
J. C. WILMOT SMITH, Esq.

R. F. MEYRICK, Esq.
E. WARDLE, Esq.
G. R. LANE FOX, Esq., M.P.

Officials.

Mr. W. CLARK, Collingham. Leeds, Clerk of the Course.
Mr. J. GODFREY LONG, Spofforth, Harrogate, Treasurer & Stakeholder.
Mr. FRANK WARD, 34, Nottingham Road, Nottingham, Handicapper.
Mr. W. SCARTH DIXON, Luton, Bedfordshire, Judge.
Mr. W. R. HORNBY, Stockton-on-Tees, Clerk of the Scales.
Mr. C. LONG, Spofforth, Harrogate, Starter.
Mr. R. MILLS, Leeds, Auctioneer.
Mr. J. D. TIPLADY, Wetherby, Secretary.

Printed and published by Henry Crossley, "News" Office, Wetherby.

Above: An interesting list of the Patrons, Stewards and Officials taken from the Easter Monday programme of 1906.

Opposite above: The Parage Ring complete with horses, jockeys and punters.

Opposite below: The Hallfield Novices Hurdle, 18 November 1965. Jockey Pat Buckley of Grand National fame, on the 66/1 outsider Ayala, owned by the hairdresser Mr "Teasy Weasey".

Above: Hurdle racing at its best.

Left: Baie Noir airborne and Santa Grand approaching the water jump during the 1966 Whit Monday Ingmanthorpe Hunter Chase.

GO RACING AT WETHERBY
for steeplechasing at its best...

Prize Winning Racing Picture. British Press Pictures of the Year Competition 1966, by Chief Photographer Bert Johnston of the Express & Star, Wolverhampton.

FIXTURES 1967/68

March :
Saturday 11th
Easter Monday 27th
Tuesday 28th

May :
Thursday 4th (evening)
Bank Holiday 29th

October :
Saturday 7th

November :
Saturday 11th

December :
Tuesday 5th
Boxing Day 26th
Wednesday 27th

1968 (Provisional)

January :
Tuesday 16th

February :
Saturday 10th

ADMISSION :		
Paddock - - -	£1.5.0
Cars to Paddock -	£1.5.0
(Each Occupant £1.5.0)	
Course - - -	4.0

For details of special rates for parties, coach parties, facilities and all other particulars apply direct to:

SECRETARY,
WETHERBY STEEPLECHASE CO. LTD.,
23, NORTH STREET,
WETHERBY.   Tel : 2035

Car and Coach Parking—FREE

Children's Playground on Popular Side under Supervision.

The course is 1 mile east of town, easily reached from main W. Riding towns, nearest being Leeds, Harrogate and York, from which good buses/trains run.

'Go Racing at Wetherby'. This Fixtures List is for the 1967/68 Season.

The Evening Charity Race Meeting on 11 November 1968, attended by the Variety Club of Great Britain. Present can be seen Matt Munro and Mrs Nina Scott who had been voted as having the most beautiful legs. The man with the moustache is Harry Swales, the then President of the Variety Club. Mr J McGhile, the winning owner, received a canteen of cutlery. Anita Harris was another personality present at this Meeting.

The modern entrance approached from the A1.

Six

The Railway

The entrance to Wetherby station on Linton Road opened in 1902. This replaced the original station on York Road. It is interesting to note that a more gracious form of transport still collected the railway passengers.

The station staff with Mr Dobson the Station Master standing nearest the line and taken when the lamps were still fuelled with oil.

This picture (date unknown), of the passenger-deserted station was obviously when the staff had time to clear the platforms of snow.

Wetherby station signal box looking towards Spofforth Hill. Standing in the doorway is G L Wetherill, who remembered seeing the first turf being cut for the new single track line from Wetherby to Crossgates Leeds which opened on 1 May 1876.

Wetherby station looking towards Leeds, c.1910. Typical of most rural stations, it is immaculately clean and well kept. Behind the main station buildings can be seen the roof of the station master's house which has since been demolished to make way for homes on Station Garth.

A quiet view of Wetherby station looking towards Spofforth Hill, date unknown.

A peaceful view of the station showing the foot-bridge and a few passengers possibly waiting for the train to Leeds.

A steam-hauled freight train takes on water at Wetherby station on its way towards Leeds, c.1960.

The Devil's Toe Nail fork just east of the station, showing a Class B.16 passenger engine and train about to enter Wetherby.

A racecourse excursion from Bradford arrives at the station on Easter Tuesday, April 1960.

The last day of Race Specials ever to run. These Whitsuntide 1963 racegoers from Leeds are about to arrive at Wetherby station.

A Class B.1 freight No. 61084 leaves Wetherby bound for Leeds after having passed under the Linton Road bridge.

A Q.6 locomotive on a work train pulling freight through Wetherby passenger station in 1960.

A forlorn looking Wetherby station on Easter Tuesday 1961, when the races and racegoers were snowed off.

Seven

Wetherby at Play

The original Drum and Fife Band was formed in the years 1869–73. Notice that whilst the band had pillbox hats they still wore their own suits.

Above: The Band at the beginning of the twentieth century with a brass drum presented by Messrs Riley Smith Tadcaster, 1878. It is believed that this was at the time of the formation of the Band.

Opposite below: This photograph taken in 1893 when the Band was invited for the first time to play at the Wetherby Agricultural Show.

Above right: Mr Dave March, the founder of the Wetherby Drum and Fife Band. In 1878 he became a member of the original brass band.

Below right: Ken Maxfield, who served Wetherby Band for over sixty years. He joined the Band aged 15 and was unique by being true to the one band all his playing life; both as a euphonium player and for many years as the Band chairman.

The Band taken in the old bandroom yard, St James Street, 1930.

The Town Band proceeding to the Gallipoli Day service in August 1949.

Cricket was established in Wetherby before 1879. The Club's first ground was south of the river, behind Micklethwaite Farm where now stands the Jarvis Hotel car park. This picture of a sombre looking team was taken early in the twentieth century.

By 1926 the Club had moved on to the Grange Park and we see here the new pavilion. Before the 1939-45 War, many famous Yorkshire players like Norman Yardley and Bill Bowes always appeared in an annual charity cricket match. In 1986 this pavilion was ceremoniously burnt down to make way for the new western by-pass of the A1.

Believed to be an early photograph of the Wetherby Cycling Club, but the location and date are unknown.

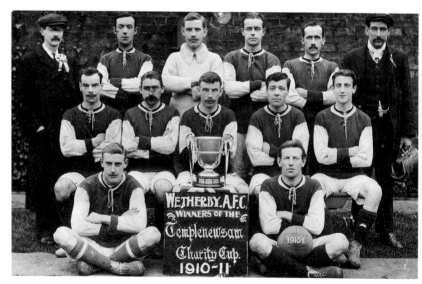

In 1902 Wetherby A.F.C. was formed as an auxiliary section of the Cycling Club, with its first ground being at Micklethwaite. Obviously, 1910–11 was a successful season with the team winning the Temple Newsam Charity Cup.

There was also an active hockey club in the town, as shown by this picture of the 1905-6 team.

Wetherby Rovers F.C. was established in 1920 and played in the Harrogate District League. They had the distinction of featuring in the Ardath Kings series of cigarette cards in the 1930s, when cigarettes cost 6d. for 10.

The earlier Bowling Club adjoining the Bowling Green Inn. Obviously from the huddle of officials, a major match is in progress.

The opening of the British Legion Bowling Club, just after the 1914–18 War, in the Quarry and showing Sandringham Terrace in the background. The Club House was also used as the headquarters of the Junior Imperial League, which unfortunately did not flourish.

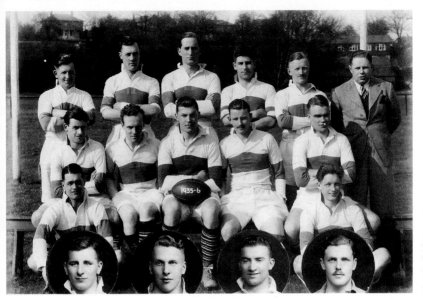

Wetherby Town Rugby Club played on the Ings up to 1939. During the Second World War they suspended their playing activities until the Club was reformed in 1966, with considerable success.

The present golf course was started in 1910 by leasing land from Lord Leconfield. The bunkers were sited by making plasticine models indicating size and location. During the First World War the Club was almost bankrupt and was only saved by the introduction of a triple mower drawn by a horse wearing leather shoes, thus saving on labour costs.

Left: Competitor, Mr R Hick, under the watchful eye of David Fowler during the Sheldon Cup competition of the Wetherby Angling Club. The Club was formed by a local ironmonger in 1933 and still has a strong membership.

Below: Wetherby County Secondary Modern School athletics team, which created school history by winning the Queen Elizabeth Shield in competition with 14 other schools. Yet another success for local youth.

Fagin's Gang from the town's Crypt Youth Centre production of Oliver in 1970.

From the theatrical beginning of the Crypt Youth Centre at St James Church, grew the Wetherby Musical Theatre Group, seen here in a very early production of *The Boy Friend*; a Society which has gone from strength to strength.

The pop singer Lulu visiting the Crypt to present the National Association's Award to Youth Clubs for the presentation of *Oliver* in 1970.

H.R.H. Princess Margaret being presented to local dignitaries of the Youth Club by Mr Ted Kilner of the Wetherby Crypt Youth Centre, on the occasion of her official visit in 1975 as President of the C of E Young People's Society.

Eight

Inns

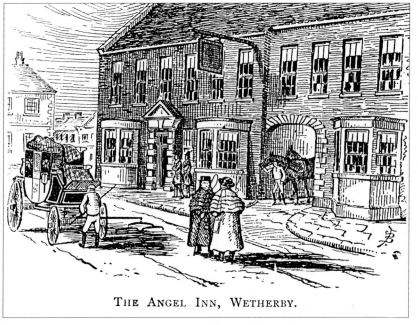

THE ANGEL INN, WETHERBY.

The Angel Inn showing a more sedate period during its stage-coach days.

The Story of the Hostelries

Until the By-Pass was built in the late 1950s the Great North Road passed through the centre of the town, along the High Street and North Street. Since Wetherby was mid-way between London and Edinburgh it is not surprising that a large number of hotels, inns and public houses grew along these two main thoroughfares and in the streets adjacent to them.

At the Great Sale of Wetherby in October 1824, a total of 12 were sold at auction. By 1837 the number had grown to 16 and by 1861 had dropped to 15.

The following is a brief synopsis of these establishments which were so important to the trade of the town.

To the south of the river bridge at Micklethwaite was the Drovers Inn (also known as the Spotted Ox), which served the cattle drovers on their way south from Scotland and the north; their cattle being watered in the river and rested in the nearby fields. Crossing the river bridge and entering the town was the George & Dragon on the right and still in existence. Almost opposite on the left was the Blue Boar (later known as the White Horse and subsequently demolished), adjoining this were the Red Lion and the Crown, both still in existence. On the High Street, diagonally opposite the Crown, still stands the Brunswick Hotel (previously known as the Devonshire Arms). A few hundred yards further to the north and on the left-hand side of the road used to stand the White Hart. Next on the right-hand side we come to the first of the Posting Houses, the Angel Hotel, which has recently been refurbished. At this point the Great North Road did a double right-angled dog's leg, with the Bowling Green Inn creating the restriction to the flow of traffic even in coaching days until its demolition in the road widening scheme of 1929. From the Bowling Green Inn northwards, the road becomes North Street where one finds the now demolished Blue Anchor public house and almost opposite on the right-hand side of the road the second of the Posting Houses, the Swan and Talbot which remains standing to this day. On the same side as the latter but further north out of town we find the last of the Great North Road public houses, the Royal Oak. In the adjacent streets we would find the Black Bull, the Fox Inn, the Three Masons and Commercial House, the Three Legs Inn and the New Inn. Currently there are 10 licensed premises in the town.

In this view of the High Street at the beginning of the twentieth century, we can see six of its hostelries. On the right the George and Dragon, the Brunswick and the Angel Posting House. On the left, the White Horse Inn, which, after the Great Sale changed its name to the Blue Boar. All but the latter named are still open.

Market Day outside the Brunswick and the Crown with a horse-drawn cart coming out of Cross Street.

The Fox Inn in Bank Street was unique since it did not belong to the Devonshire Estates, hence it was not recorded in the Sale Document. Without doubt this photograph shows the staff of the Fox together with the uniformed telegraph boy. The inn later became a lodging house.

Above and below: Two pictures looking northwards from the Angel, clearly show how Briggs' shop and the Bowling Green Inn created the Great North Road bottle-neck. Both were demolished in the 1929 road widening.

The Angel, c.1910. Note how this Posting House has made the transition from coaching to the motorist. Opposite and next to Moons is the now closed White Hart, with the Crown and Red Lion lower down the street.

A fine view of the Crown on the left and the Brunswick, previously the Devonshire, advertising their Magnet Ales.

The New Inn and Bank Street at the beginning of the twentieth century. Hiding behind the lamp is the sign for the now closed Fox Inn.

One of the few older pictures of the historic Black Bull Inn which is the fourth building from the alleyway.

An artist's impression of the Swan and Talbot Posting House during its coaching days.

The Swan and Talbot, c.1910, with townspeople and some staff standing outside. The ornate gas lamps over the door is worthy of note.

Nine

Transport

Fairground haulage stood in the Market Place, showing the chairoplane drive, accommodation caravan and a heavily loaded trailer.

Nellie (Mrs Mawson) from Kirk Deighton with her mute mule Necromancer, named after the Derby winner of that name. This tough old lady 'led coal' to the houses between Wetherby station and North Deighton until she was 77 years old.

A decorated carriage and pair stood outside the Angel Hotel, most likely awaiting the bride and groom.

Two heavy goods carts after picking up their loads from the York Road railway goods depot, Wetherby's original station, built in 1847. It closed to passengers in 1902 when the Linton Road station opened. This area was known locally as Dolly Field.

The Westerman family hauling timber, location unknown, possibly en route to the town sawmill.

As far back as 1905 the motor car was used for political purposes, as seen at the 1905 By-election.

Two fine old buses in the Market Place, date unknown.

One of the first cars in the town, a Humber, c.1904, owned by Dr J A Hargreaves, outside his surgery at Wetherby House in the Market Place.

The two Hargreaves children playing with a child size Governess cart.

A 1922 belt-driven Triumph model "H" motor bike of the type used by army despatch riders.

Two fine cars standing outside Ingmanthorpe Hall. The open topped car is a 12hp German Alder of 1909 vintage. The other is a 35hp 1907 Talbot Landaulette.

Dalby's garage in North Street with a selection of vehicles, c.1912. The front two are Model T Fords. The owner, F W Dalby, is standing on the Dalby truck's running board.

This lovely Victorian Casket, built in 1898, started its life as a horse-drawn hearse. Later modified to fit this Austin motor chassis, it was interchangeable with a private ambulance body and continued to be used by Dalby's garage until 1950.

Above: Car racing at Wetherby Grange in 1936; the driver is Mr George Dracup. Exact details of the car are not recorded.

Left: An Albion lorry outside Robinsons transport depot in Deighton Road. Note the white painted wartime flashes on the front mudguards which assisted recognition during journeys made in the black-out.

Ten

Houses of Note

The barracks of the Yorkshire Hussars at Micklethwaite. As can be seen, they are now in a state of dereliction. In their earlier days they must have presented an imposing sight as people approached the town from the south.

Ingmanthorpe Hall, home of the Montagu family and originally mentioned in the Poll Tax returns of 1394 under the name of Robert De Ros.

An aerial view of Ingmanthorpe showing the extent of the very fine Hall and the cricket ground.

Members of the staff at Ingmanthorpe, c.1910, which at that time was owned by Captain F J O Montagu, who was Lord of the Manor of Wetherby and owner of the racecourse until 1920.

The Meeting of the Hunt at Ingmanthorpe Hall, date unknown.

Hill Top House was originally built during Queen Anne's reign and belonged to the 6th Duke of Devonshire. It passed into the Hudson family in 1871 and was eventually modified to the house as seen in the picture.

Priest Hill, so called after the Augustinian Monks who were the first recorded owners. It then become the home of the Rhodes family who owned the brewery and for a time it was also the home of the Tiplady family. In 1850 it was a boys' boarding school with 27 boarders.

When the earlier Stone Dene workhouse ceased to operate in 1861, the new workhouse was built on Linton Road in 1863 at a cost of £5,000. Before closing in the early 1990s, it became a home and hospital for the mentally subnormal.

Wetherby Union Workhouse Infirmary, c.1930, used over the years as a hospital and accommodation for the Matron and nursing staff. Like the workhouse building it is currently undergoing redevelopment as apartments.

The imposing Hallfield House, the home of Colonel Tetley of brewing fame. At the time of going to print the house is still standing. The house originally had substantial parkland attached , which was later developed as a large modern housing estate.

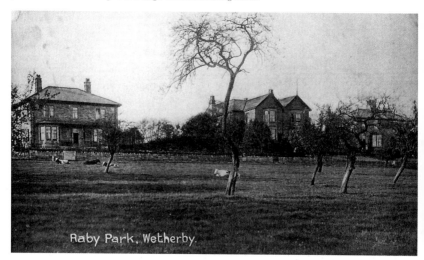

Raby Park, Wetherby.

Raby Park was a significant housing development built as a result of the railway coming to Wetherby and named after the Revd William Raby.

Wetherby Grange c.1910. Originally known as Micklethwaite or Bielby Grange. The first hall was built in 1666 and was entirely encased in the Georgian conversion seen here. The house was for many years the home of the Gunter family until it was finally demolished in 1962.

A rear view of the Grange showing the lawns and gardens.

The Lodge of Wetherby Grange. Sited at the southern entrance to the town, this elegant frontage can still be seen.

The original stables of the Grange modernised with accommodation for jockeys above the stables. The Gunters were very keen trainers and horsemen and also ran the Bramham Moor Hunt.

The Grange stables, c.1910, being used to house fine motor cars. The one on the left is a 50hp Mercedes of the 1907/8 era. The car in the centre is most likely a 1907 4 cylinder 40/45hp Mercedes, whilst that on the right is a 1907/8 20hp Martini.

Lady Gunter at the wheel of the 20hp Martini with attendant chauffeur.

Left: Castlegarth, previously known as Pelham House was owned in the 1870s by John Bradley, a well-known Catholic. Due to there being no Catholic church in the town, he allowed Mass to be said in the loft above his coach-house.

Below: Playing croquet on the lawn in front of Castlegarth in more gracious days.

STOCKELD PARK, WETHERBY,

Stockeld Park was the home of the Middleton family who were staunch Catholics. The present house is eighteenth-century and retains much of its palladian character. It also has a very fine detached private chapel. At the time of the Great Sale the then Peter Middleton purchased land within Wetherby adjoining his estate.

Rear view of Wharfedale Lawn which was the home of Mr Kelk (a local businessman), and his wife. When they left, it became a home for elderly ladies run by the West Yorkshire County Council.

No.7 in the Market Place was the home and surgery of Dr E P Gibson and later Dr J A Hargreaves. It continued as a practising surgery for over 75 years. How sad it must have been when the lovely Regency iron railings had to go to help the 1939-45 war effort.

The house at the corner of Sandbeck Lane in which the Second World War fighter ace, Sq Ldr James (Ginger) Lacey D.F.M. and Bar spent his formative years.

Eleven

Celebrations

This Wetherby-to-Boston Spa bus was decorated for the celebrations of the Silver Jubilee of King George V in 1935. The driver of the Dennis is Mr Percy Etherington of Wetherby.

Queen Victoria's Diamond Jubilee celebrations in 1897. Notice the horse-drawn fire engine and the very large banner of the Wetherby Buffaloes Friendly Society, but most of all note how little this part of the Market Place has changed.

The folk of Wetherby unite to commemorate the coronation of Edward VII in 1902. Note how everyone wore a cap or hat of some description.

Lavish setting for Wetherby waterworks luncheon party for 300 guests held in the Town Hall ballroom on 1 August 1900. The catering was by Mrs Gaythorpe of Wetherby's Angel Hotel. This was to celebrate the arrival of piped water to the town. The fire brigade obliged with a cascade of water over the Town Hall.

A Weslyan Methodist Whitsuntide procession through the town, although the exact date is unknown. This was always an important annual occasion.

A large turnout for the 1909 Boxing Day Meet of the Bramham Moor Hunt. Notice the number of people who attended in their carriages.

The Beagle pack meets on Wetherby Bridge, c.1904. Note what a good view there is of the now demolished Bishopsgate.

The Scout Guard of Honour parading in the Market Place prior to leaving for the christening of Lord Lascelles at Goldsborough Hall near Knaresborough, c.1922/23.

Church parades were a regular part of the Scout and Guide movement in the thirties. Seen here are the guide troops marching along Church Street in 1936, to the accompaniment of the Scout Band.

Water carnivals were a feature of the town's celebrations. Here we see a magnificently decorated punt.

Four ladies suitably dressed with their decorated cycles during a water carnival.

A large group of people in fancy dress, some on horseback and others with decorated cycles. Sadly we do not know what the occasion was.

A coach and four advertising Bertram Mills Circus in the Market Place, c.1930. In previous years the Bostock and Wombwell Circus performed each year in the Market Place. Considerable anxiety existed in case the lions and tigers should escape from their cages. It must have been quite a sight to see the horses and even the elephants being taken down Scott Lane for watering in the river Wharfe.

A group of Wetherby folk collecting money in front of the Town Hall for the Leeds General Infirmary during a 1919 fete.

In the thirties garden fetes were a popular form of celebration for both fund raising and commemoration. This particular one at Castlegarth, the home of Mrs K D Colley, was held in July 1935 in aid of Wetherby and District Nursing Association.

A group of Wetherby children in fancy dress, for the 1945 Victory procession and celebrations.

The Morris Dancers come to town. Unfortunately there is no record of what the celebration was for.

Celebrations on 8 July 1990 to mark the 750th anniversary of the granting of the Market Charter. Town Crier for the day, Jack Winterburn, presents the Lord Mayor of Leeds with a copy of the Charter.

The town community constable, P.C. John Tatterton, oversees the proceedings dressed in the uniform of an early Peeler, c.1830.

Twelve

Wetherby at War

The War Memorial which stands on the
bridge parapet at the entrance to the town.
Notice the large number of wreaths laid on
that occasion.

The Leeds Territorial Rifles in Wetherby, c.1905, parked up in the Market Place. The opening at the far side of Thorntons is Scott Lane.

144 Battery of the Royal Field Brigade of Artillery at muster for inspection at the entrance to the Market Place during the early part of the 1914–18 war.

Two members of the 155 Brigade standing outside Wetherby house in the Market Place. Only three people in the photograph are known. From the left they are Miss Hargreaves, Captain Stanley Waller and Mrs Hargreaves, the wife of Dr J A Hargreaves.

The Coal Owners 155 Brigade crossing Wetherby bridge whilst leaving the town with their horse-drawn limbers and 18 pounder guns. It is believed that this was their final departure from the town on their way to the Western Front in July 1915.

The Royal Field Artillery on parade for the last time before leaving Wetherby for Ripon.

The Wetherby Territorials say goodbye to their loved ones at Wetherby Station on being called up in 1914.

Troops of the Royal Artillery water their horses in the Wharfe below the bridge, c.1915.

Royal Field Artillery on muster in the Market Place for the last time in 1915.

An interesting group of First World War Land Army Girls who worked on local farms.

The 84th Voluntary Aid Detachment (V.A.D.) who served at the Officers Convalescent Home at North Deighton Manor. Often their duties involved taking their charges to the Royal Bath Hospital in Harrogate.

Right: The Coal Owners, 155 West Riding Brigade Royal Field Artillery who were billeted in Wharfedale Brewery, march down the High Street. It is interesting to note that the town council agreed to loan them the town band's instruments.

Below: The dedication of the town's War Memorial on 24 April 1922 by the Earl of Harewood.

Above: The town adopted the minesweeper H.M.S. *Selkirk*. This started through a crew member contacting a member of the St John's Nursing Division. The people of Wetherby provided two of their main needs—thick woollen jumpers and string gloves.

Above: The local St John's Ambulance Brigade being instructed in Air Raid Precautions training in first aid and gas drill during the Second World War.

Right: The nursing staff of the Wetherby First Aid Post taken with St James Church in the background during the Second World War.

Opposite below: Wetherby's own naval training ship H.M.S. *Ceres*. In 1942 it was named H.M.S. *Cabot* and when the first crew arrived the rum ration could not be given, since the perimeter fence was not secure. Somehow this information found its way to the German propagandist Lord Haw Haw who broadcasted that the H.M.S. *Cabot* had been sunk, much to the amusement of the local people. In 1943 it was renamed H.M.S. *Demetrius* and shortly after become H.M.S. *Ceres*. The farewell parade took place on 14 March 1958.

The town's group of Volunteer Rescue Workers taken in 1941. They did a fine job complementing the other rescue services.

Officers and N.C.O.s of 'C' Company (Wetherby and District) 11th West Riding Battalion of the Home Guard, photographed in 1944.

Thirteen

The Workplace

The archway into the Brewery, bearing the cross of
the Knights Templars on each side. This is believed
to be the site of the Templars' first building in
Wetherby.

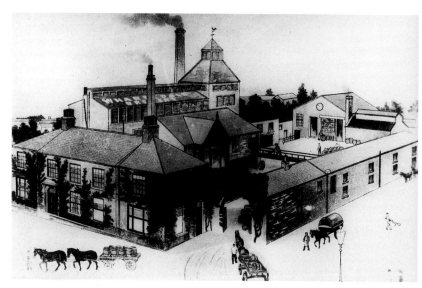

An artist's impression of the Wharfedale Brewery. Over the years it supplied beer to many of the town's inns. It ceased brewing during the early part of the 1914–18 War when it provided billets for troops and stabling for their horses. Later it became Oxley's mineral water works and in 1943 provided Coca Cola manufactured from concentrates for the American forces.

The staff of the Wharfedale Brewery including many young boys, who in some industries were employed to read the delivery notes for the drivers who were often unable to read.

Right: The staff of the *Wetherby News* outside their offices. The gentleman in overalls on the extreme left is Mr Henry Crossley, the owner. In contrast on the far right with collar and tie is the Editor, Mr James Clay. In 1857 the *Wetherby News* was printed in premised at Bridge Foot by Mr Crossley senior before moving to larger premises adjoining the Angel Hotel in 1872. Prior to the *News* taking over these offices they had previously been the old Wetherby Courthouse and at a later date the post office plus the office for the transmission and receipt of telegrams.

Below: Crossley's Printers entered into the town's life in the 1850s under their founder Henry Crossley senior. The firm produced the *Wetherby News* along with four other local papers. Here we see the very busy compositors at work.

The gasholder is clearly visible in this picture. Wetherby had its first gasworks by 1845 and by 1852 the installation of gas lighting was achieved.

J Fox, Saddlers and Harness Makers displaying their goods at their premises in the Market Place (where Lunn Poly now stands). Later they moved to Northgates.

Mr Fred Garton, a farrier and shoesmith for over 50 years. During his many years connected with the racecourse, he shod many big race winners.

Whilst this is a recent picture, the scene depicting the auction of farm animals has changed little.

The premises of J C Hanson, shoeing and general smiths in York Road, c.1945.

An interesting insight into the workshop of local tinsmith Hugh Hall, showing his work-bench where he would have made and repaired varied agricultural and domestic pans and containers.

The early premises of Sandbeck Garage (now Sandbeck Motors Ltd.) founded in 1943. At first occupying only half of this building, by 1947 the company had taken over the whole building and has continued to grow.

F Johnson and Sons have been builders and builders' merchants from this same site for over three generations.

Above: A collection of workmen at Westermans' timber yard and sawmill, which was located near the weir.

Left: Teasdale and Metcalfe, a local firm of agricultural building manufacturers. Founded in the early 1920s they became a major employer in the town. Their reputation developed to such an extent that not only can you see their buildings in Yorkshire but throughout Great Britain.

The joinery workshop of W H Field, which is a veritable museum as well, due to the owner's interest in historical artefacts.

A true rural workplace showing farmer Cyril Skirrow milking cows by hand with his well-dressed wife looking on, c.1930.

On Spofforth Hill at Quarry Bottom where the Leconfield Court flats now stand, there was a large bulb and tomato farm. This picture shows a tulip forcing shed with Miss Hilda Johnson watering and Mrs Minnie Maskill picking.

In 1956 Farnell's, the international electronics equipment manufacturers, started from humble beginnings in ex-W.D. huts on Wetherby's York Road industrial estate. They employed a small team of seven manufacturing and repairing testing instruments.

By 1963 business had improved to the extent that Farnell's found it necessary to move into a purpose built factory on Sandbeck Way where they employed 40 people. With further extensions over the years the company has become one of the town's largest employers.

Another of the town's manufacturers are Arville Industrial Textiles who manufacture specialised industrial fabrics for many highly technical applications.

Synthetic fibre cone winding machines, within the plant at Arville Industrial Textiles.

Fourteen

Churches and Chapels

The Calvinist chapel built in 1817 at the top of New Street (now Victoria Street). This is one of the oldest complete chapel buildings left in Wetherby. It ceased to function as a chapel around 1835, until it became the home of the Primitive Methodists whilst their new chapel was built in 1874.

WETHERBY CHURCH.

St James's church, c.1905, the foundation stone of which was laid by Mr Quinton Rhodes on the 1st April 1839. He was a wealthy man who not only donated the organ and bells, but also his efforts were largely responsible for the money being raised to build the church at a cost of £4,000; the stone being quarried at Collingham. The later extension to the chancel can be easily seen by the elevation of the roof.

The nave and chancel of St James's church taken c.1909.

A view of Church Street showing the tower of St James's church without its original pinnacles, which had become unsafe. These were removed in 1939 and replaced with the present day capstones.

The Christian Army meeting house in Bank Street, dated 1916.

Left: The Wesleyan chapel in Bank Street built on land purchased by Mr James Wiggins at the time of the Duke of Devonshire's Great Sale of Wetherby in 1824, for a price of £720. Before 1824 there was a Methodist meeting house in Fox Yard where the Silver Band's room now stands. At the beginning of 1829 the Methodist Trustees purchased the land and the chapel was built ready for opening by October of that year. The exterior remains unchanged to this day.

Below: The inside of the Wesleyan chapel; unfortunately there is no date recorded.

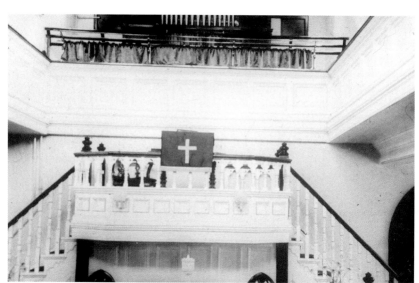

The Primitive Methodist chapel in North Street, built in 1874 following their vacation of the old chapel in New Street (now Victoria Street). The 1874 chapel has since been demolished.

In 1873 three acres of land were purchased in Hallfield Lane as the town cemetery, with these two fine chapels being built near the main gates.

Prior to 1882 the Catholic community was served by a priest from Sicklinghall, celebrating Mass in a loft over a local coach-house. Then in May 1882, Bishop Robert Cornthwaite of Leeds opened St Joseph's church. The building on the left of this picture is the original church and was used as such until the new church and extensions were opened in 1986.

The inside of the old Catholic church before modification in 1986.

Fifteen

Townspeople

A study of peace and tranquillity. This view shows the rear of Bishopsgate, an area now demolished, seen by people as they entered Wetherby from the south.

John D Tiplady, born 1853 and died in 1925. Through partially sighted from an early age he succeeded in gaining entry to Oxford University. On his return to Wetherby he held numerous public offices including the position of Company Secretary to the Wetherby Steeplechase Committee. He is best remembered, however, for being the first Clerk to the Parish Council from 1894 until his death.

Henry Crossley senior. A true Wetherby entrepreneur and founder of the *Wetherby News* in 1857. The paper was printed in premises adjacent to the Angel Hotel. By 1860 its circulation was 2,000 copies and still growing. By 1871 he was the proprietor of four local weekly newspapers.

This old picture shows two of the local blacksmiths, Josh Benson and George Precious. It is said locally that both were so punctual that if you saw them crossing the Market Place on their way to work either in the morning or after lunch, everyone knew what time it was without looking at the Town Hall clock.

"The cleaning's done" or is it just starting? Miss Harriet Robinson standing at the rear door of Fairview House in Baden Terrace.

Right: Mr James David Hudson came to Wetherby on purchasing Hill Top House in the 1870s, following a successful career as a provision merchant during which he had a considerable Anglo-American trade connection. His introduction of the Hudson family to Wetherby had a major influence on the town.

Below: Major Joseph H Hudson, a prominent figure in many areas of public life, during which he held leading positions in local government at parish, town, district and county levels and as a magistrate for 40 years. Seen here enjoying tea with Barbara Castle.

Left: Mr Hugh Hall who managed the family ironmongers and tinners business for many years. Shown here whilst still working at the age of about 90 years.

Below: The official opening in 1952 of the shelter in the Garden of Rest by Alice Richardson, whilst many well-known local people look on. The shelter was presented by Charles Edward Whitaker, a local school master.

Mrs Barker is a study of Victorian elegance sitting outside her home in Church Street, c.1896.

Dr J A Hargreaves, the Medical Officer of Health from 1894 to 1939 and the owner of the first motor car in the town. His persistence against all odds for a clear pure water supply paid off when piped water came to the town in 1900.

Dr Edmund H Lodge, the Medical Officer of Health to the town during the years of the Second World War, seen her with Mrs Lodge just prior to being made a Knight of Grace and Mrs Lodge a Dame of Grace of the Order of St John, in recognition of their long years of dedication to the Brigade.

Right: Sq Ldr James (Ginger) Lacy D.F.M. and Bar, Wetherby's own Second World War ace fighter pilot. During the Battle of Britain he shot down more German aircraft than any other fighter pilot. He is also accredited with shooting down the *Heinkel* III which bombed Buckingham Palace.

Below: Harry Mason B.E.M. Born in 1897, he died in 1988 at the age of 91. During his long life he was the Superintendent of Wetherby Cemetery for 65 years until his retirement in 1985. In his early years as superintendent, he was released by the Parish Council to be deputy Chief of the Fire Service which at that time was under the control of the Parish Council.

A Lucky Pig.

You may push me
You may shuv
But I'm hanged
If I'll be druv
From WETHERBY.